Paul Sams is a practicing property Solicitor actively involved in residential, residential and commercial development with niche specialisms in leasehold enfranchisement matters plus equity release.

Louise Uphill is a practising leasehold enfranchisement specialist Solicitor handling all aspects of lease extensions, collective enfranchisement and niche leasehold issues.

Covid-19, Residential Property, Equity Release and Enfranchisement – The Essential Guide

Covid-19, Residential Property, Equity Release and Enfranchisement – The Essential Guide

Paul David Sams
LLB Hons (silver badge in Cycling proficiency)
Solicitor
Specialist in all matters Conveyancing both
Residential and Commercial

Louise Clare Uphill LL.B (Hons)
Solicitor
Specialist in Leasehold Enfranchisement

Law Brief Publishing

Published 2020 by Law Brief Publishing, an imprint of Law Brief Publishing Ltd
30 The Parks
Minehead
Somerset
TA24 8BT

www.lawbriefpublishing.com

Paperback: 978-1-913715-13-7

PREFACE

Thank to our colleagues and spouses for assisting us in putting this book together. The law is correct as of 14 June 2020.

Thanks Mam for putting up with me and not leaving me out for the bin men as I think I probably deserved sometimes when I was growing up. What you and Dad sacrificed for both Craig and I was far more than most parents would do. Particularly given what Craig and I could be like (and sometimes still are!). – Paul

I would like to dedicate my contribution in this book to my parents. Without their constant, unwavering support and encouragement I would not be the person I am today. I would like to thank my husband for putting up with me during lockdown, he hasn't seen me much as I have been glued to my desk but he has helped me through and made sure I ate and stayed hydrated! My thanks too to Paul and Dutton Gregory, for taking a chance and hiring me, I look forward to growing the firm's enfranchisement offering together. – Louise

Paul Sams
Louise Uphill
June 2020

CONTENTS

CHAPTER ONE
INTRODUCTION

Congratulations. If you are reading this then you have not been taken out by the Zombie apocalypse raging all around us at present. However it may be that you are the last human left on earth. If so double congratulations as you will have this book to keep you entertained for the rest of your natural days as you await rescue by aliens.

In all seriousness the world has never faced something so uniting in one way but dividing in others as Covid-19. Never before have Governments collectively taken decisions to effectively stop their respective economies in turn causing huge financial hardship to their people. In the United Kingdom the respective national and regional Governments/Assemblies have worked together (to some extend) to limit the movement of their citizens to try to stop the spread of what on the face of it is a virus that takes it victims so viciously.

The speed at which everything has happened has taken a lot of people by surprise. I myself was at a conference in London in early March when I think the concerns were coming to the form that something quite drastic was going to happen. I don't mind admitting I thought it was all a "fuss" over nothing. A glorified version of the common cold, a mild dose of flu with some bed rest, chicken soup and a nice cup of tea would soon clear up. How wrong I was in that belief.

For my sins, and for leaving the Partners annual retreat to "spend a penny" at an inappropriate moment I fear, I sit on the Management Board of my law firm. Meetings in the run up to "lockdown" were focused on the growth of the firm. We were not foreseeing that anything could stop us save nuclear war. We had not counted on a respiratory virus the likes of which no one has seen before.

Meetings went from looking to expand to finding the best way to consolidate. Cuts and savings needed to be made. Staffing needed to be reviewed. The whole way of working needed to be adapted. It needed to be done quickly. No time for a leisurely review. We needed to be ready.

In advance of the lockdown being announced on Monday 23 March 2020 by Boris Johnson my firm already had everyone working at home. The few people who went into the office to deal with post had discovered the phrase "social distancing" as had the rest of the world. My firm and many others had people working from home before but few in what I like to call "Traditional" law firms had required their entire staff to work remotely.

To say we did some "field testing" is true and we checked that the entire accounts teams could work remotely for instance rather than all being huddled together in their corner of the office. The rush to ensure that everyone had a laptop took place as of course we had a lot of people with them but I dare many firms to say they obtained expensive computer equipment for even their most junior members of staff. All done without too much fuss to ensure we were all ready for inevitable to "stay at home, protect the NHS and save lives".

During this time we had people who really wanted to complete transactions. I can understand it. If they wanted to move from one place to another, had found their dream property and had an inkling that they were about to have to stay in one place for some time surely now was the time to do so.

I have to say one of my favorite stories during this time is the firm whom we completed a transaction with the Friday before lockdown commenced. They stated on their email footer they were closing for two weeks from that Friday. When asked why they said it was so they could prepare everything for their staff to work remotely. I am not sure if I was their client that I would be happy to hear that. Clients, particularly residential conveyancing clients who are transformed from meek and mild easygoing folk into foaming at the mouth rabid animals because they had to leave a message because you dared to cheat on them by speaking to another client when they called, do not care what your internal issues are. They are paying for a service and they expect to get it. Let's face it, we lawyers would be the same if we were in their shoes.

So we all got ready across the UK it seems to work from home. The Government then threw a lot of businesses and law firms somewhat of what our American cousins refer to as a "curveball". The Government Job retention scheme or furlough as it is colloquially known was announced on 20 March 2020.

This was, and I hate the phrase as it is used too much but in this case I will make an exception, an unprecedented action. Millions of UK citizens would be paid by the state to help their employers. The legal profession was no exception to this and tough, sometimes heartbreaking decisions had to be made. I won't lie – choosing who to keep in place was one of the hardest things I ever had to do.

However the announcement of furlough and the rush to ensure that it could take place for the conveyancing world in itself caused issues. I like to think my firm got it about right in that we had an orderly handover to the staff that were remaining on the front line. It was not perfect but on the whole was ok. Our people make us. Never a truer phrase then during these difficult times.

Of course not all firms were as organized and our clients have had to suffer from what frankly have been some horrendous situations with other organisations. Another favourite story from this time is a major conveyancing firm whose main switchboard number diverted to an automatic message suggesting that unless you had exchanged on your matter there was no point calling to which the message then swiftly ended. No alternate number to call, no chance to leave a message, no suggestion you look at their website, no email address to try, no destination for you to send a pigeon to with a message strapped to its foot, absolutely nothing. Certainly not client care from them but mere bordering on criminal neglect.

Some have adapted to this brave new world. I frankly love being able to work at home. I am set up with dual screens, can work, as I am now typing this section myself at home in the garden with a nice chilled glass of something alcoholic close at hand, that being my wife's glass of course. Some have struggled. I am fortunate to have my family with me. Some who live alone have felt isolated and my heart goes out to them. Some have simply struggled with the change because it is such a change to their routine. For the first few weeks of lockdown I was terribly ill with flu symptoms. I don't know if it was Covid-19 but whatever it was it was not pleasant. We self-isolated and I am forever grateful that my wonderful wife Sarah looked after me as she always does.

Well in this book let's take a look at the changes to the world of Residential Conveyancing, Equity Release and Enfran-chisement. Residential conveyancing I think has changed for the better. The need for original documents has changed ever so slightly. Client meetings face to face can be handled by "screen time". Identification checks can be dealt with in a more efficient and proficient way. I will take you through in the following couple of chapters the changes that have taken place and look at some of the specific tips, comments and general musings I have to offer about conveyancing in this brave new world.

The biggest change we will look at is in relation to Equity release. The constraints of having to meet the borrowers in person have been replaced with video conferencing which I have been advocating for so long I think my voice has etched a tattoo of those words on my derriere. I will look at the major changes and warnings that need to be adhered to with the changes now in force.

Finally we will look at Enfranchisement. So at this stage of this chapter at least I will hand you over to Louise for her comments on this. Louise is the real enfranchisement specialist. She is younger, thinner and far better looking than me too. However I beat her in being far more verbose…

Whilst I can't promise that enfranchisement is the most riveting subject in the world, I will provide you with an overview of how Covid-19 has impacted this niche area of law and how enfranchisement experts like me have had to adapt to a new world which includes the serving of notices electronically.

I joined my Firm at the end of January 2020 and so didn't really have a great deal of time to get to know my new colleagues (and the IT system) when I suddenly found myself working at home, alone, save for my husband and the dogs! I had left my last firm to work separately from my husband (as we met at work) and now here we were, working together again, in the same building at least!

Like Paul, I had been to a conference in London in early March, hosted by the Association of Leasehold Enfranchisement Practitioners (ALEP) where we joked and laughed as we pretended to air kiss and bump elbows to say hello, all the while singing happy birthday as we washed our hands. Not in a million years did we think that it would have been the last time we physically saw each other as an association, but I suppose, stranger things have happened haven't they?!

Due to the way in which files had been handed over from various parts of the Firm, some files were hard copy and others were electronic. This presented a number of problems because not everything was available to me immediately. Clients had received out of office messages from my colleagues who were on furlough leave and because clients were perhaps on furlough themselves, and the world was in a state of panic, they wanted an immediate answer to their questions. In those early weeks of lockdown there were many late nights and weekends working to maintain the service levels, as after all, clients didn't really care for the internal politics, they just wanted their deal done.

In a broad sense, enfranchisement is a mix of property litigation and residential conveyancing with a hint of corporate law and a dash of counselling for extremely anxious clients. It can be difficult to happily marry the immoveable deadlines with the fast-paced world of conveyancing and it takes a certain type of person to be able to balance the two without dropping the ball. In my case, it just makes my hair go grey!

Well, enough about me, you are here to learn about how Covid-19 impacted the way in which the enfranchisement world now functions. Here I will discuss how ALEP have once again been at the forefront of enfranchisement by helping its members to adapt and adjust to working in this new electronic environment. We will explore the issues faced by practitioners during the Covid-19 pandemic and provide useful tips on how to work more effectively in this brave new world.

CHAPTER TWO
RESIDENTIAL
CONVEYANCING
ISSUES

Sadly, some people you speak to will say that the words above always follow each other, residential conveyancing = issues. Harsh but being in that field of work myself I should probably feel maligned by that statement. Sadly, too often it is true though.

On the back of the fact that too often the statement is true it does tend to have a propensity to become a self-fulfilling prophecy. A recent example I have had is with a new client who instructed in relation to a purchase. After instruction she contacted me rather concerned that she said her sister-in-law had used my firm for her conveyancing and there was "nothing but issues". Being the person with whom the "buck stops" at my firm I spoke to my now client about it and asked if she knew any reason why. She did not but gave me her sister in law's name and I assured her that I would welcome a call from her sister in law to discuss her concerns.

Well on checking the file the final item saved into the system was an extremely pleasant email to my colleague Rebecca thanking her for all her help. She made the point of saying how unlucky the sellers had been with their conveyancer who had caused all the delays and issues. Needless to say my current client's sister in law has not called me to discuss. However it goes to show how one can be guilty by association.

So what have been the big issues in my experience with Covid-19 and residential conveyancing? Well there are many. In the next chapter I will discuss and examine why so called "Covid-19 clauses" are perhaps not the perfect solution to potential delays in the chain. I would like to use this chapter to look at the practical issues that conveyancers have had on a day-to-day basis. Some, I have the solution for and some, well I will let you use your imagination.

So lockdown began, conveyancers were furloughed. Some firms did this diligently. I would like to think mine did. Making sure that those who were going on furlough understood what that entailed, making sure they informed their clients as to whom was looking after their work moving forwards, how to contact the new person handling their file and most importantly (at least I think) a reassurance that the file would be looked after well.

The furlough scheme has seen in general the most senior people remain at firms and the most junior, less experienced and dare I say lower earners placed on furlough. This has not been the case with every business and certainly not the case with every law firm but business continuity is and was essential. Those who remained at work needed to rapidly take on at least one and in some cases two people's case loads.

Now in usual times taking on someone else's work on top of your own would frankly fill people with dread. Double the work? Less administrative support? Having to work from home instead of the office with all the modern conveniences it brings? To be honest at times it is not the office banter I have missed the most but the air conditioning and the amazing zip tap we have in the kitchen at work that produces boiling water for the copious amounts of green tea I go through.

From my own experience I was extremely lucky that I took on the case load of my colleague Traci whose files were in immensely good order. Of course there were something that I would have done differently. They were issues of style over substance. I am a huge believer in people expressing their own individuality when they write or speak. You will no doubt see this in the different tone and style that Louise and I adopt throughout this book. Clearly her way of doing things is what some would consider more shall we say, expected from a practicing solicitor where mine is rather like that of a frustrated stand-up comic.

However taking on someone else's work partway through a transaction can be traumatic for all parties, clients, lawyers and introducers. I found myself quite often in the first week assuring clients that actually yes I did know what I was doing, apologizing for not having their express permission to furlough whomever they had been dealing with and often trying to find out who was dealing with a matter now on the "other side" of various transactions.

I will tell you what I told my team. The first week is all about triage. It was a case of working out where matters were at, who had what and being reassuring to all the parties involved on a matter including our colleagues. Teamwork has been key throughout this. I have to say that I have always worked closely with my clients and those who kindly have referred work to me over the years but since Covid-19 has hit us I have never worked closer with them. Teamwork has been key.

As I have said I will look more closely at the legislation and so called Covid-19 clauses in the next chapter but for now would like to look at some of the practical solutions I have been working with to get matters to progress throughout this rather fraught time. I would stress that I nor my colleagues nor the property industry as a whole have developed anything say as revolutionary as nuclear fusion, a pill to make you thin (my prayers will be answered one day for the same) or built a rocket that can take us to Mars. What we have done is adapted to the situation to use technology that we all always had but to be honest neglected to us.

As a profession I think that this time of worldwide crisis has in a way forced us all to use technology more. I reckon we are five to ten years ahead where we would have been with the same because frankly we have had to be. I have typed this book myself (save for Louise sections, crikey if she wants a writing credit she can get tapping those keys as well!) but there are still a huge amount of people out there who are dictating on to a cassette tape. Yes I know they still exist. In the twenty-first century when I can ask my smart speaker to play any track I want (you can't beat Tiffany's "I think we are alone now") how can it be sensible for one person to dictate (awful words isn't it) to someone on a cassette (for younger readers this is ancient recording device) a document or letter. Why not do it themselves, use speech recognition or better still a case management system that can do most of what they want for them in advance.

The number of firms I have contacted even now who state that "Mr or Mrs so and so, (not allowed to call the person they work with every day by their forename), is just going to dictate something for me to send over to you". Why doesn't Mr and Mrs so and so do something novel like do it themselves, email me with it or something very revolutionary such as pick up the telephone and call me. It was frustrating before the crisis and it just down right irritating to me now.

One of the first issues I realized that needed to be addressed at work was to make sure everyone was ok. Yes I know not something that perhaps would be at the top of someone who runs a business' primary concerns when cash flow becomes even more of a focus but as I will keep saying our people make us. Speaking to people on the telephone is no substitute for actually seeing that person in the flesh, obviously with clothes on, I don't run that sort of establishment.

Video conferencing was something I have used for years. Every Sunday I would use the same to contact my Mother who lives three hundred and fifty miles away to allow her to see her grandchildren, I am this minor irriatation she has to put up with to get to see my children whom are now more important than me. Using video conferencing at work was a novelty to some but not really for me.

You see (pardon the pun) I have been lecturing other lawyers on various legal issues for years using video conferencing. To think, in January 2020 I thought the most difficult task facing the conveyancing world was the issues stemming from rent charges on freehold properties under section 121 of the Law of Property Act 1925. How times have changed!

However my familiarity with video conferencing has helped and in fact I think improved the conveyancing process. For starters I can check in on the team via video call to allow me to see their facial expressions which is far more revealing that a telephone call. It, more importantly, has allowed clients to see my stunning good looks (not too many comments yet that I bear a startling resemblance to a vet from a popular UK soap opera set in a Yorkshire village) and interact with me from the comfort of their own homes.

No having to travel to our office, no arduous car journey, no "cheeky" drive through lunch or dinner on the way home and more importantly what a benefit to the environment. During these troubling times I keep having to look for the positives.

In part I chose the car I decided to buy a few years ago because the dealer sent me a personalized message before I purchased. I loved that personal touch and wanted to bring it in for my clients but always found a reason not to. Covid-19 has forced me to use video conferencing with clients and it is great. I have been able to use it to such great effect. For example with a residential developer client I was able to discuss an option agreement plan with him, his planning expert and land manager all on one screen. We could look at a plan that was to be attached to the option and then all agree the tweaks there and then. If they had come to the office it would have been nice for us all to meet in person and have a coffee. However the time in travelling, clearing diaries, making the coffee then back and forth over the plan would have taken more time.

One thing that has particular irritated me during this time is the reliance on so many firms wishing to carry out a simultaneous exchange and completion. The whole idea about exchanging contracts is to provide certainty. The role of the lawyer in the conveyancing process is to provide certainty. There have been many firms for years who have adopted a chaotic approach to the whole business that they seem to think that simultaneous exchange and completion is the "only way to go". I expect that is because they have no system in place or belief in their ability to deal with it any other way.

Now I am not saying that someone should never exchange and complete on the same day. There are circumstances where that has to happen. However they should be the exception to the rule not the norm. There have been many firms I have dealt with over the years (yes I am old) that have always seemed to prefer a simultaneous exchange and completion. Oddly those firms always seem to be the ones that end up in trouble with the regulators at some point.

The argument that many put forward to not exchange in advance of completion is somewhat counter intuitive. They say they can't be certain they will be able to complete. As I have stated above the point of exchanging is to provide certainty to parties in the first place. The reasons stem from "my client may fall ill" and "the mortgage offer could be withdrawn". Well yes their client could fall ill but is that a reason not to exchange when they clearly have funds lined up?

The other reason put forward I have heard as mentioned above is "the mortgage lender could withdraw their offer". Well, newsflash to those who did not know this but a lender has always had the right to do this. A huge amount of conveyancers seem to think that if a mortgage offer is issued then it can't be withdrawn. Covid-19 has not changed this reality so why exchange before the pandemic but not now? As you can tell I get quite worked up about this issue so best I move on. And breathe.

We will look at the Government and property industry guidelines in depth in the next chapter but I would like to consider now the innovation in signing of documents during the time from when Covid really hit us in March 2020 until now. Practical solutions have had to be found to what we all took for granted before.

Conveyancing has always been very paper driven. Now I am in a minority I fear in that, I hate paper. I appreciate that most of you will be reading these words in a paper backed version of this book thinking the man is crazy. You won't be the first to suggest that but I honestly do hate paper.

I have been an advocate of having dual screens to work with for a number of years. I like being able to have two plans open at one time or having a document to compare to another. I also do my own typing and very occasionally cook. I say this because those are apparently unusual things for someone to do in my profession but they work for me and my costs have always been good which is what one is always judged on first.

Covid-19 has forced many to abandon paper and rely on their case management systems more, assuming of course they have one. I have had to chuckle at far too many firms who have asked if I can send copies of documents they sent to me in the first place as they have "left their file in the office" and need to check something. I feel at times that I have been their assistant as they cannot do anything themselves.

Surely Covid-19 and home working must be showing to those firms who dare I say it are behind the times, that to keep their clients and be able to function then a "paper-lite system" such as my firm runs is key. We only keep the original documents we have to. Keeping down the paper really helps not just clients but the firm themselves. Cabinets for files take up storage space. Office space is generally calculated by the square foot or meter as opposed to residential property which depends on how many bedrooms a property has. Let the conveyancing world embrace less paper. It is more efficient for clients, better for the environment and will save each firm a fortune in paper let alone the postage involved. "This is the way we have always done it" simply will not work moving forwards into this brave new world.

Speaking of paper, the handling of contracts for sale has certainly been given a "push in the right direction" due to the Covid-19 crisis. Electronic signatures are not new. They have been used in the wider world for a considerable period of time. From ordering clothes from an online retailer, ordering a new mobile telephone from an internet retailer or signing a lettings agreement, these have all been carried out for what seems like an age by using online signatures.

However we luddite conveyancing lawyers are slowly starting to adopt the same. Electronic signatures are amazing. I can send a document to a client via email clearly marked up as to where to sign. No longer do I have to tolerate people signing in the wrong place on a contract, marking it with the date, changing the few special conditions and my favourite of all time when a client returned their contract with the shopping list for his girlfriend's Christmas presents. At least he said it was his girlfriend's Christmas present list.

Some people worry about electronic signatures being forged. The system I use and many others use or use equivalents that do the same, provide a security certificate so you know where it was signed by way of the IP address being used. Signatures can be forged but the electronic tracking although not infallible is far more secure and precise.

Most firms have been happy to accept electronic signatures and I have been happy to share the "secrets" of the technology with other firms as well. It is in my client's and my own interest to have the other side of a transaction able to progress matters as quickly as they can. As an aside I am grateful to a great number of individuals in other firms who have acted very sensibly during these harsh times, more on those who have not later in this book.

The signing process for documents has been relatively straightforward. Documents such as contracts are fine because they do not need a witness, albeit clients always ask if they do it seems even though the instructions are always fairly clear. Witnessing documents has become a tad trickier because of social distancing.

The first thing to remember with a witness is we always tell people their signature should not be noted by a relative. The simple reason behind that stems from the signing of a Will. A relative cannot be a witness neither can a beneficiary as there is that element of doubt that the Will might have been "interfered with" or undue influence may be in play – see more on this in the Equity Release section of the book later on. I keep trying to get you to the turn the pages don't I? If you would like a legal reason check out *(Seal v Claridge (1881) 7 QBD*

516 at 519) "a party to a deed cannot be a witness to the same".

One of my favorite tales about a witness comes from a client on the Isle of Wight. Don't get me wrong I love the place (save the roads) and the people but some (not me) may say this is typical for the Island. Many years ago a client of mine from there called me and said "Can my Mum witness my signature?" I explained not as she was a relative. She replied "OK but can my Dad?". My response of "ask your Mum?" I think may have confused her. I never did find out if she asked her or not though.

So how to witness a deed during measures of nationwide social distancing is, pardon the pun, indeed tricky. There are some ways this can be achieved though. Firstly there is the method I like to call "knocky nine doors" which was something nefarious children did when I was growing up. Not I though. In essence your client would approach their neighbour's house having called them first to say they needed a witness to a document. The client would greet their neighbor through the protection of a closed window. They would proceed to sign the document. They would then post this through the neighbour's letter box. They neighbor would then witness and post it back through the letter box. Everyone washes their hands that has signed the paperwork and the job is complete.

Variations to this method include the video witness where say I would call a client, they would sign the paperwork before me on a video call that I would record then the same would be posted back to my office for me to witness. In addition some "non-high street" lenders were happy to accept a third party signing paperwork but a solicitor witnessing and recording the whole thing via video conference. As I said earlier the benefit (we have to look at the positives and remain optimistic) of Covid-19 is that it has forced our technology forward around five to ten years. We have been at war and during war innovation is always enhanced.

One of the other methods of witnessing documents is the now infamous if I can call it that "Mercury method". Sadly this is one of those sections of the book where I feel I have to apologise as I am about to quote some case law. Sorry. The case in question *is* R (on the application of Mercury Tax Group and another) v HMRC [2008] EWHC 2721 *(Mercury).*

In short this was a case that decided that wet signatures did not actually have to be used for property documents. HM Land Registry then adopted the terminology for their purposes. Now as all conveyancers know original documents need to be on your file for exchange and completion. These can range from transfers to mortgage documents of all kinds. Conveyancers need the original on file but ninety nine times out of one hundred the originals are literally on file with scanned copies going to HM Land Registry.

Very few mortgage lenders ask for original mortgage deeds albeit some do but woe betide you if you did not receive an original back in the first place. However on 6 May 2020 HM Land Registry agreed that they would accept temporarily at least, the "Mercury" signing method. All the where's and why for's are set out in the very helpful Land Registry Practice Guide 8 – execution of Deeds.

Again some more law, with a few exceptions (section 52(2) of the Law of Property Act 1925), a legal interest in land cannot be conveyed or created without a deed (section 52(1) of the Law of Property Act 1925). The exceptions include:

- assents, which must be in writing but need not be executed as a deed (section 36(4) of the Administration of Estates Act 1925)

- leases taking effect in possession for a term not exceeding 3 years at the best rent which can be reasonably obtained without taking a fine (section 54(2) of the Law of Property Act 1925)

Now you should all know what a deed is but for those that need their minds refreshing:

To be a deed a document must:

- be in writing

- make clear on its face that it is intended to be a deed by the person making it or the parties to it. This can be done by the document describing itself as a deed or expressing itself to be executed as a deed 'or otherwise'

- be validly executed as a deed by the person making it or one or more of the parties to it (section 1 of the Law of Property (Miscellaneous Provisions) Act 1989)

Now that we are clear on that we need to be clear on how the same should be signed. To be validly executed as a deed, each individual must sign the document. "Making one's mark" on a document is treated as signing it (section 1(4) of the Law of Property (Miscellaneous Provisions) Act 1989). The signature must be on the document itself in the space provided and the words of execution must name the signatory or otherwise make clear who has signed the document. For obvious reasons, the signature ought to be in ink or some other "indelible medium". I know some clients over the years who have suggested that may as well be signing in their own blood.

HM Land Registry helpfully set out the steps as follows:

- STEP 1 – Final agreed copies of the transfer are emailed to each party by their conveyancer.

- STEP 2 – Each party prints the signature page only.

- STEP 3 – Each party signs the signature page in the physical presence of a witness.

- STEP 4 – The witness signs the signature page.

- STEP 5 – Each party sends a single email to their conveyancer to which are attached the final agreed copy of the transfer (see STEP 1) and a PDF/JPEG or other suitable copy of the signed signature page.

- STEP 6 – The conveyancing transaction is completed.

- STEP 7 – The conveyancer applies to register the disposition and includes with the application the final agreed copy of the transfer and the signed signature page or pages in the form of a single document.

- STEP 8 – The application is processed by HM Land Registry following standard operating procedure.

There of course come exceptions to the rule (there have to be do there not as all good rules have exceptions) being:

- A deed that effects one of the dispositions referred to in section 27(2) and (3) of the Land Registration Act 2002 these of course being:

    ○ (2) In the case of a registered estate, the following are the dispositions which are required to be completed by registration—

    ○ (a) a transfer,

- (b) where the registered estate is an estate in land, the grant of a term of years absolute—

- (i) for a term of more than seven years from the date of the grant,

- (ii) to take effect in possession after the end of the period of three months beginning with the date of the grant,

- (iii) under which the right to possession is discontinuous,

- (iv) in pursuance of Part 5 of the Housing Act 1985 (c. 68) (the right to buy), or

- (v) in circumstances where section 171A of that Act applies (disposal by landlord which leads to a person no longer being a secure tenant),

- (3) In the case of a registered charge, the following are the dispositions which are required to be completed by registration—

- (a) a transfer, and

- (b) the grant of a sub-charge.

- A discharge or release in form DS1 or form DS3.

- Equivalent deeds in respect of unregistered land.

- A power of attorney other than a lasting power of attorney – I don't expect Conveyancers to be dealing with these though to be honest – one for our Private Client colleagues

So in short a rather convoluted way to deal with things but a way that HM Land Registry and will expect. By the time you have read this book they may have even processed my applications from 2019.

Now enough about the conveyancing world in general. Let's have a look at some specific ways of how transactions have proceeded during Covid-19 and the lockdown period along with my musings on why some firms and convey-ancers have it completely wrong.

CHAPTER THREE
COVID-19 CLAUSES AND THE CONTRACTURAL POSITION

The standard conditions of sale in residential property transactions (and commercial ones as well) were designed to stop the long arduous free fall with contracts that existed before. The thought process was that if all contracts had a standard set of conditions within them that would speed up the conveyancing process. In theory this is correct. However the Law Society over looked the fundamental failing in all lawyers, lawyers being lawyers like to amend things. They do this because they think on the whole they are the cleverest person in the room. I always work on the alternative basis of that, clearly I must be the stupidest so I try to be measured in what I say and do. Sometimes that works.

I happen to be writing this chapter on a Saturday and a solicitor in another practice and myself were having a very helpful exchange in trying to ensure our respective clients can exchange in the coming week. I therefore credit her with the following phrase when I mentioned what I was up to do (as you do) which I think all residential property lawyers should pay heed to. It is this "mess with the contract at your peril".

Once upon a time I saw a former colleague alter the standard conditions of sale on a purchase to try and protect her clients deposit position if the matter went abortive after exchange. She removed one standard condition to cover this but did not think of the remedy conditions that exist if completion does not take place. Some careful maneuvering was needed to resolve the same. I am generally good at coming up with solutions to issues that arise, some of them I amaze myself with to be honest but let me make myself clear, I would rather not have to do so. Might seem strange but I would really like an easy boring life. I really would, one day I may get my wish.

So Covid clauses. By this what do I mean? Well when Covid-19 hit us all with a harsh reality of what it would mean to our society the Law Society produced reasonably regular updates to its members, particularly those involved in residential conveyancing.

The Law Society provided guidance based on the Covid-19 situation. Some firms I found during the, what I shall call very serious months of the crisis, simply refused to complete any transactions. In some cases breaching their clients express instructions. Why they took such a unilateral decision I am not sure. What I know for certain is that firstly they are likely to be severely damaged both financially and in the eyes of their clients as well as potential clients. Given the Law Society's grave warning that up to seventy one percent of legal firms will suffer severe financial hardship possibly resulting in closure by the end of 2020 I for one found this attitude extremely bizarre. For what I can acknowledge are intelligent people then lawyers as a whole have little business sense or people skills. Not everyone falls into that category but if you ask lawyers I bet most would agree. Secondly at no point have the Government or the Law Society told people not to complete property transactions or prevent clients from moving.

The Law Society's draft clause we will look at below but they set out some general guidance. It was made clear that the suggested clause was not suitable for every transaction and was actually for use in a limited number of transactions. Nor did the Law Society recommend that the clause was used or endorsed for use. It was designed to highlight issues which could legitimately justify delaying completing transactions where contracts had been exchanged.

I have to say that an awful lot of firms have shown some great deal of what is the word, oh yes, idiocy in their dealing with the same. I had one firm send me a rather vanilla Covid-19 clause. There was no real reason for it. The property my client was selling was vacant. The buyers were living with one of their parents. My client had arranged for the property to be professionally cleaned the week after she left. However the firm acting for the buyer insisted they had to have a Covid-19 clause. I agreed to ensure the matter proceeded as my client needed the funds. The firm in question then said that now the Covid-19 clause had been agreed their "policy" was only to exchange and complete on the same day. When I made what I thought was a fairly obvious point, why a Covid-19 clause when there was no risk, I was told that clearly I did not know what I was doing! Scary that their clients entrusted people like that to act on their behalf with the most expensive item they had ever purchased. I can't see that firm surviving the inevitable recession we are facing in 2020.

Sorry some real law again. The standard conditions of sale at standard condition 7.2 provides that if parties do not complete on the date agreed in the contract then compensation should be paid. Standard condition 7.4 provides that if a notice to complete has been served and completion has not taken place within the terms of the same then the buyers deposit can be forfeited. It is rare and in the thousands of transactions I have only had to do it once. Oddly enough when the property in question sold again following the first abortive sale I thought the second buyer was going to fail to complete as well but they came through, eventually.

The Law Society recognised there was a real risk of this happening as some of the media were producing some fairly alarming reports early in the crisis. The recommendation was for us all to work together in the profession to make sure buyers and sellers were protected. Some went above and beyond in doing this whilst some I feel failed their clients spectacularly in some cases. Deferring completion (which I did for a few matters) and recession were options that were advised to be considered. Of course this would only work if all parties agreed. In a chain of many properties this could be an issue. In fact quite often it was.

The Law Society provided a variation agreement which I have referred to as a Covid-19 clause throughout the pages before (and after this). In reality that variation agreement was to deal with the situation where contracts had exchanged. The majority of Covid-19 clauses I have seen and have dealt with relate to clauses that have been added to contracts prior to exchange rather than varying contracts in existence. Every firm has one or has people within their firm tweaking the same. The Covid-19 clause is 2020's "Overriding Interests form", you know that fairly pointless form that a lot of firms insist on having which your client will sign having not read or understood.

Covid-19 clauses should reflect the following general principles as set out from the Law Society and of course you should discuss the same with your clients. It is for you to advise your clients not actually tell them what to do although that may be very tempting to do at times. The provisions of any Covid-19 clause require good faith on the part of all parties.

In such a clause it was important to cover what could be considered a delay provision. From the ones I saw they revolved around if a party fell ill with Covid-19 or if the Government implemented legislation preventing house moves taking place. Some clauses attempted to provide an exhaustive list of reasons for delaying completion. I did joke with one firm they had missed a couple of reasons such was the length of their delay event matters. When they asked what I pointed out Elvis being discovered in a local supermarket or alien invasion were not in there.

Any Covid-19 clause needed to be clear what it was trying to achieve. Some people failed badly in realising that. Such a clause needed a clear mechanism in place as to what a delay event was, what the delay should be, what a long stop date should be and most of all it needed to be agreed by all parties. The issue of course has been when a chain of transactions has been in place then how do you get everyone in a chain to agree a Covid-19 clause or worse still a Covid-19 variation clause to vary the completion date.

This crisis has shown us the best in people, crossing the road when out to allow people by to keep our two metre distance, actually speaking to those people you see out, praising those key workers who make a difference to our lives rather than celebrity worship and appreciating our families more. Sadly I have also seen the worst in people. Clients trying to take advantage for their own financial benefit has probably been the worst. Covid-19 variation clauses allowed this to become more of an option for them.

Now moving forwards what are the likely outcomes following on from Covid-19 clauses. Well I think that a general clause for force majeure (Act of God) is likely to be added to the special conditions of sale for both residential and commercial transactions. The issue being what will class that as being?

Lawyers are used to providing certainty. Well I actually I think often these days they are used to provide professional indemnity insurance if things go wrong but I am a cynic. If we start adding such wide-ranging clauses to contracts what certainty do our clients have? This might be an advantage to certain parties. I have had a few clients call me during the crisis asking what their options are to have them "get out" of what they have agreed to purchase. In fact I have seen that many times over the years. This particularly happens with "off plan" purchases as buyers often have a chance to change their mind about a purchase when there is a longer gap between exchange and completion. They have had a change of circumstances, moved job, lost their employment or more commonly fallen out with that special person they were purchasing with. When this has happened I have always done what I can for them but always point out that they did enter into the contract being informed exactly what they were doing.

As you can probably gather from my tone, I am not a fan of Covid-19 clauses. I fear some lawyers just use them because they have a "crowd mentality" and have seen others use them so fear they must. So I would reiterate what I repeated from my peer in another firm "mess with the contract at your peril".

Now enough about the negative effects of Covid. Let's take a look at one of the positive stories to arise from this crisis in relation to the changes to how solicitors should and can handle equity release matters.

CHAPTER FOUR
EQUITY RELEASE –
THE CHANGES FOR
THE BETTER?

For the past few years the equity release financial sector has been the fastest growing part of the financial sector. In 2019 it was estimated that borrowers were releasing eleven million pounds per day via equity release borrowing. That is four billion pounds a year. That is enough for you to purchase the Royal Navy's latest aircraft carrier HMS Queen Elizabeth with change to buy some aircraft for it, well three by my reckoning. Still very impressive to moor up and show to your friend though.

So quick recap for the uninitiated, what is equity release? Well to put it briefly it is when someone over fifty five years of age borrows money from a financial institution against a property. It used to have to be their main residence but that has been relaxed to some degree. Usually it is paid by way of a lump sum, no monthly repayments take place. This money is only repaid when the property is sold or the borrower enters long-term residential care or the borrower has died. The maximum amount of money that borrowers can take tends to be no more than sixty percent of the value of their current home. Interest is charged at a fixed rate which is on a compound basis meaning that if someone were to borrow say

£100,000.00 at a fixed compound interest rate of 3.5% they would owe the sum of £141,059.88 in ten years' time. In twenty years' time they would owe £198,978.89.

Now I have written a whole book on equity release so I don't plan to regurgitate that all in this chapter (you could of course just buy the book – all royalties go to charity after all). What I want to look at are the changes that the Covid-19 crisis has brought to the equity release industry. They are things that in most cases I have been advocating for many years. The fact that the changes are listed as temporary I hope will allow the industry to show that they should actually remain.

For an area of borrowing that deals with the elderly who are generally held by society to not be as technologically advanced (I don't hold that view mind you) I have to say I have always thought that equity release has been very pro-gressive. The way the model of borrowing works is rather sensible and the Equity Release Council make great efforts to ensure that all parties participate in an ethical way. It is a shame that not all such trade bodies are so proactive.

Once Covid-19 hit the Equity Release Council and the industry as a whole took some very positive steps to ensure that equity release matters could continue relatively unaf-fected. The first step was with lenders. When the announcement was made by the Prime Minister that people should stay at home this had a profound effect on all of us. A fundamental of lending money is that the lending institution wants to ensure that the property over which they are securing a substantial amount of their money is suitable for that purpose. Valuations have generally involved the surveyor going to a property to ensure that it is firstly there and secondly that it is in a suitable state of repair for the loan in question. How does a surveyor carry out their role when they could not visit a home owned by someone else?

Desktop valuations. By this I mean that a surveyor will provide a valuation based on limited or indirectly sought information where a full inspection of the property in question has not taken place. In essence the surveyor arrives at their expert opinion as to the value of the property from their desk. Now these are not a new concept as they have existed for many years. In fact I always liked the sound of their predecessor, "drive by valuations". I still can't shake the image I formed in my head of a surveyor speeding down the road to the property in question then performing a handbrake turn whilst snapping some pictures of the property with their camera rather like a gang related shooting.

Lenders were quick to realise that to keep their business running they needed to adapt. The same applied to advisers. They were always required to meet the borrower to explain the position to them and to ensure that equity release was the correct option. For some there are many other options they should explore first and the advisor as the potential borrower's first person they discuss this with in some depth will often be able to steer that person to a better path.

Not being able to visit people at their homes or somewhere else such as the advisor's office has allowed advice to be provided by other means. By this I mean telephone and video conferencing has come to the fore for the financial advisors who have the specialist knowledge to discuss equity release with borrowers. Now you might wonder why people may want to borrow money during the Covid-19 crisis. Well life still goes on and if they have a need that need must be met.

Now financial advice forms part of the initial process of equity release but it is the element provided by solicitors that has the process complete and monies in borrower's pockets. Often I have referred to the solicitor's role as the gate keeper to the funds.

I have to say that the Equity Release Council really do deserve praise for acting so quickly as they had their guidance ready and available at least a week before the Prime Minister made his announcement that we should all stay at home. Well what was the main thing they suggested do I hear you say? Well the role of the solicitor was always to arrange for them or another solicitor employed by them as their agent to see the borrower in person. The amendment provided for by the Equity Release Council was that this physical face to face meeting was no longer required.

Why face to face do I hear you say? What was the point in that any way? It is not needed for any other type of mortgage advice in general to so why equity release? All good questions. These stem from the Equity Release Council rules that all lenders and solicitors that act on equity release matters agree to follow when advising borrowers.

Rule 8 has always required that a solicitor advising on an equity release mortgage and providing the "solicitor's certificate" has met with the borrowers at least once face to face in person. By solicitor's certificate I am referring to the certificate that must be signed in all matters to confirm that the borrower has been advised by their solicitor of certain keys facts.

Those keys facts being:

- That they have considered discussing the fact they are taking an equity release mortgage with their heirs and beneficiaries

- That they are aware that by taking the equity release loan they will be reducing the amount of money available to their Estate when they pass away, particularly if they have the misfortune of dying shortly after taking out the loan

- That they need to be aware that by borrowing the funds they could be affecting the benefits they may be claiming now or claiming in the future

- That they are aware that by taking the equity release loan they have a duty to maintain the property in question in good repair and to ensure that the property is insured fully

- That they have security of tenure to remain in the property provided they don't breach the mortgage conditions

- That they are satisfied that the financial advice they have been provided by whomever the advisor is who has arranged the loan has provided them with the correct information

The solicitor's certificate is to be signed by the solicitor and countersigned by the borrower at the time they meet. Now this level of advice is not a requirement for say a residential mortgage for a high street bank. It is almost unheard of for a high street lender to now require a borrower's signature to be witnessed by a solicitor albeit when I first started in the profession that was relatively commonplace for a large number of lenders. Showing my age.

Rule 8 though has some fairly specific criteria that other mortgage products do not that are unique to equity release mortgages. Firstly these are for the solicitor to confirm that the borrower has the mental capacity to enter into the equity release mortgage. Secondly that the borrower is not under undue influence or duress to enter into the equity release mortgage.

Now these are actually pretty onerous conditions placed on a solicitor. Some would say there is no way I should be commenting on or acting in relation to equity release mortgages when I have such questionable dress sense and a choice of football team to support that causes me much anxiety. However these two criteria are somewhat unique when it comes to the obligations placed on a solicitor acting for any type of borrower. I have always found it ironic that, shall we say more experienced borrowers who may have had many mortgages over the years, should have a higher level of advice than say first time buyers who have never borrowed money before.

The criteria to meet a client face to face has been in place since 2014 hence before to some extent the solicitor's certificate was not required to be counter-signed by the borrower. During the Covid-19 crisis the Equity Release Council took the bold decision to relax on a temporary basis the criteria to see a borrower in a face to face personal meeting.

Previously the points of the solicitor's certificate had been considered unsuitable to be verified by video call. How was the solicitor to check that someone was not in the background influencing the answers given? How did they know that the person was not suffering whilst on the call to benefit some third party hidden in their home? What if the person on the call was not real and merely a computer generated image? You may mock the last point but a video blogger in China was revealed in 2019 to be projecting an image of her looks. Her image on screen bore no resemblance to her image in the flesh.

The relaxed requirements of a face to face meeting have been supplemented though with more stringent criteria for the acting solicitor for the borrower to meet. The Equity Release Council have rightly pointed out that during this time of economic uncertainty that the elderly may be targeted by unscrupulous family and friends looking to influence them in a negative way to borrowing money that they do not need for the benefit of others. Solicitors are reminded to ask what the money is for and to check that reason with the financial advisor who arranged the equity release mortgage in the first place.

The revised guidance requires the borrower's solicitor to run through the solicitor's certificate as normal via video call. The solicitor must ensure that in relation to point 1 regarding discussing the fact that by taking the equity release mortgage then the Estate of the borrower will be reduced to ask that if they have not informed their relatives, heirs and beneficiaries that they plan to take the equity mortgage why they have not done so. It is also clear that during this meeting via video call that the solicitor should ascertain who the witness to the mortgage deed will be. As this will be signed and witnessed away from the solicitor the solicitor needs to obtain identification documents for the witness as well.

Once the video advice is given then a written report should be sent to the client along with the mortgage deed for signing. The Equity Release council have recommended that a copy of the attendance note made from the video call or perhaps if possible a copy of the recording of the meeting should be made available to the borrower. The Council are also at great pains to reiterate that the acting solicitor should make it clear that social distancing measures should be observed when the mortgage deed is signed.

Now I have run courses on equity release up and down the country for many years now. I have always advocating making sure that a full attendance note is made of the meeting with an equity release client as if there is a problem in the future and heaven forbid a claim is made for some reason against the firm they work for then that attendance note will provide evidence of what went on. However with a video call that is recorded what better evidence is there than that.

Many years ago I went on a course run by a chap advising on the Wills and Inheritance Quality scheme who suggested that advice on Wills should be given by two solicitors at the same time with the meeting being recorded. I remember balking at the idea of the cost involved. Well with the advent of technology we have the ability to make that reality happen for very little cost. In fact video conferencing tends to be at a cheaper cost as we all don't have to travel around.

What I hope I have shown in this chapter is that equity release has adapted during this time. Far better than some elements of the law in other fields. It is an opportunity to grasp and I actually hope these temporary measures are modified into the new way of working as I think there is a great benefit to clients as well as the solicitors involved not to mention the environmental benefits.

Well now, I am sure you are getting bored of my irreverent musings now so in the next chapter let me hand you over to a legal expert in her field. Louise will take you through the changes to how enfranchisement matters have been working whilst I take a break to wash my hands for the twenty fifth time today and to apply some more hand sanitiser.

CHAPTER FIVE
ENFRANCHISEMENT

Leasehold enfranchisement is the umbrella term given to statutory lease extensions and collective enfranchisements (or purchase of freeholds) under the Leasehold Reform, Housing and Urban Development Act 1993 (as amended) ("the 1993 Act"). The term can also cover informal lease extensions and purchase of freeholds, Right to Manage claims and Right of First Refusal also known as section 5 sale of freeholds by landlords. Here I talk about all the above and how Covid-19 and the enforced lockdown has affected this area of law.

The purpose of this chapter is not to go into the complexities of the leasehold enfranchisement legislation, instead, it is to explore the issues faced by practitioners during the Covid-19 pandemic and to provide practitioners with tips on how to work more effectively in this brave new world.

In my opinion the biggest change in enfranchisement practice during lockdown has been the way in which statutory notices are now served. Whether this is a temporary or permanent change remains to be seen but, in my experience, it has a largely positive impact on the enfranchisement process (if adequate safeguards are put in place). So, let us discuss the major changes in the way we are now working.

The Current Position

Under enfranchisement legislation, all notices must be "given" by being served on the intended party in their hard copy original form. Section 99(1) of the 1993 Act states that *'any notice required or authorised to be given under this Part shall be in writing; and may be sent by post".* The case of *Cowthorpe Road 1 – 1A Freehold Ltd v Wahedally [2017] L. & T.R.4,* whilst only a Country Court decision states that because a notice must be sent by post, it can be inferred that a hard copy must be received. His Honour Judge Dight further concluded that it is a requirement that most notices must be signed and that any notice sent by email could not be an original as it could only ever be a copy. Indeed in this case, which concerned the service of a section 21 counter notice in a collective enfranchisement claim, the claimants had only provided a postal address as the address for service and so the solicitors were only authorised to accept service in physical form at that stated address.

The requirement for a hard copy notice sent by post is certainly true of most property notices in England and Wales. The legislation that deals with the service of notices was enacted long before electronic mail and electronic signatures were envisaged. However, the Law Commission, in its report dated 4th September 2019, stated that electronic signatures can be used to execute documents provided that the signatory intended to authenticate that document.

So where did this leave us in during the Covid-19 pandemic? Most offices were closed, and all staff were working from home. How were practitioners going to ensure effective service of notices during the countrywide lockdown?

The ALEP Protocol

Enter ALEP who launched the ALEP Protocol for Service of Initial Notices and Counter Notices During Covid-19 Pandemic on 30 March 2020. ALEP is at the forefront of the enfranchisement sector and quickly provided its members with helpful guidance and practical steps to ensure that the sector could continue to run smoothly during the crisis.

Whilst the Protocol was not mandatory, and could only be imposed if both parties agreed, ALEP encouraged its members to adopt the Protocol where possible. This ensured that its members were able to continue providing a quality service for their clients. Importantly for clients, whilst Covid-19 had stopped the world in its tracks, it had not been able to stop residential lease lengths depreciating.

Although the ALEP Protocol did not intend to remedy the issues of effecting valid service under the 1993 Act, it was, and still is, extremely helpful in helping practitioners find a way to deal with these issues.

The ALEP Protocol states:

1. *"Wherever possible, members should seek to agree, on behalf of their clients, a reasonable extension of time for the service of any Counter Notice under s. 21 and 45 of the [1993] Act. The length of the extension should recognise the difficulties experienced with gaining access to properties for valuers, preparing valuations, and the delays in investigating the tenant(s) right to acquire the freehold.*

2. *Where applicable, the parties should endeavor to agree that service of an Initial Notice by electronic means will be sufficient for the purposes s.13 and 42 of the [1993] Act. Service by electronic means will usually involve an email sent to the email address of the ALEP member (as agent for the recipient) with a PDF of the signed Initial Notice.*

3. *Where applicable, the parties should endeavor to agree that service of a Counter Notice by electronic means will be sufficient service for the purposes of s.21 and 45 of the [1993] Act. Service by electronic means will usually involve an email sent to the email address of the ALEP member (as agent for the recipient) with a PDF of the signed Counter Notice.*

4. *ALEP does not purport to give advice on the form and effect of any such agreements. However, the agreements should generally be accompanied by a statement that (save as agreed), the parties waive (i) the requirements as to service of s. 13, 21, 42 and 45 notices (as the case*

may be), (ii) the time periods specified by s. 21(1) or 45(1) of the [1993] Act and / or (ii).

5. *[The] Protocol will expire on the same day that section 55 of the Coronavirus Act 2020 expires."*

As soon as ALEP released this Protocol, I know I certainly felt slightly more relaxed. In the first week of lockdown the Law Society had released guidance for conveyancers but there was nothing that I could find that helped with statutory deadlines where notices had to be served in hard copy with a wet ink signature.

ALEP Protocol in Practice

How did this work in practice? My initial concern was that my counterpart solicitors on the other side wouldn't be so keen to adopt this Protocol as it could prejudice their landlord client's position if a deadline was moved by agreement rather than it being missed.

I was originally trained as a landlord solicitor back in 2007, when most solicitors weren't aware of, or at the very least were not fully versed in enfranchisement. As a trainee, I had been taught all of the ways in which to use the 1993 Act to best protect a landlord client. Allowing a deadline to be missed would enable the landlord client to obtain a higher premium for the lease extension. Fast forward three years and I had packed my bags and headed to London and to a more tenant focused firm where being proactive was key to never missing those deadlines. I quickly learnt that there are nice landlords and there are not so nice landlords in this world. Why then would a tenant's solicitor allow a landlord extra grace to serve its counter notice.

What I have learnt over the past 2 months is that in most cases ("most" being the operative word) parties just want to get the deal done. In these uncertain times, leaseholders need their leases extending and landlords need the income. I was therefore pleasantly surprised by my fellow practitioners in the industry in adopting the ALEP Protocol.

In practice, when acting for leaseholders wanting to serve a section 42 notice, I establish very early on, who the landlord's and managing agents are so that I can obtain an email address for them. The first point of call is the ground rent and service charge demands as legally, the demand must provide an address for service in England and Wales pursuant to sections 47 and 48 of the Landlord and Tenant Act 1987. The demands themselves provide contact details for either land-lords or leaseholders and so a quick search of the internet resulted in an email address being obtained.

Most professional outlets have some sort of Covid-19 statement on their websites driving all correspondence in to their office electronically. In fact, as Paul mentions above, most organisations had furloughed their junior staff and so in most cases, I have direct access to the senior professionals working during the pandemic. In my email to them, I would explain about the ALEP Protocol and seek their permission to serve statutory notices electronically.

To my surprise, most reciprocated and granted permission for me to serve my client's notices electronically. Where I was dealing with solicitors and requesting their permissions, I was pleasantly surprised by the willingness by all to get the transaction effected. Some offered me time extensions to serve counter notices and others set out precisely how they would accept service by email.

What follows therefore, are my top tips at getting around the hard copy service requirement whilst adopting a more modern and efficient way of working in line with the ALEP Protocol. Whilst some may see this as overkill, in my view, there is too much litigation in the leasehold enfranchisement sector surrounding service of notices and so it is better to err on the side of caution than to risk ineffective service.

1. Ascertain whether the office of the intended recipient is open and able to receive post (as most offices are operating a skeleton service during lockdown);

2. Discuss the ALEP Protocol with the recipient and seek to agree its implementation between the parties;

3. Ensure there is direct permission for service of every individual electronic notice that is being served;

4. Serve an electronic PDF scanned version of the hard copy signed notice and confirm this in the covering letter;

5. State in the covering letter that the notice is served via email as previously authorised and state the authorised email address;

6. Request a delivery and read receipt when serving the electronic notice;

7. Request that the recipient confirm receipt in writing within 4 working hours;

8. Record all receipts and permissions in the client file;

9. Unless otherwise agreed, send the original hard copy notice by first class or recorded delivery post on the day that electronic service is effected.

On the basis that the above points are considered, and if requested, a hard copy of the statutory notices follows by post, an effective service of the statutory notice can be affected by email.

What about other statutory notices?

The ALEP Protocol didn't necessarily deal with all notices that need to be served under enfranchisement legislation because if it did, it would have been overly complicated and would have taken a lot longer to produce. ALEPs members needed easy to follow guidance, and fast. However, it goes without saying that the ALEP Protocol can be and has been applied to other enfranchisement notices.

Whilst in lockdown, I have successfully served and accepted various notices including notice to deduce title and notice requiring statutory deposit, pursuant to paragraphs 2 and 4 of schedule 2 to the Leasehold Reform (Collective Enfranchisement and Lease Renewal) Regulations 1993, by email. I have also served section 6 and section 8 notices under the Landlord and Tenant Act 1987 in relation to the right of first refusal. In all cases, my counterpart solicitors have been agreeable to proceeding this way and if I were to reflect, I would say it has had a profound effect on the speed of the transaction. Let's not forget that whilst in lockdown, the postal system has been slow and unreliable and so in finding a new way to work, we have been able to be more efficient with transactions (not to mention the added environmental benefits of using less paper).

Deadlines and the 1993 Act

Enfranchisement legislation and particularly the 1993 Act carry multiple deadlines which, if missed, can adversely affect a tenant's ability to extend the lease or a landlord's ability to receive a higher premium than that proposed by its tenant.

It is prudent therefore to touch on some of the deadlines discussed by the ALEP Protocol to explain how the Protocol has helped legal and surveying professionals to navigate enfranchisement law during these unprecedented times.

Where a qualifying tenant has served a section 42 notice, to extend his or her lease, or the requisite majority of qualifying tenants have served a section 13 notice, to purchase their freehold reversion, then in both cases the landlord has a period of two months from service of the said notices to serve its counter notice pursuant to section 45 or section 21 respectively.

Failure to serve a counter notice within the time table laid down by the 1993 Act (or as stated in the section 42 or 13 notice) will entitle the tenant(s) to either extend their lease or acquire the freehold on the terms as stated in the respective section 42 or 13 notices. This could have dire consequences for a landlord because notoriously, a tenant will propose the lowest premium that can be calculated in accordance with the 1993 Act. A landlord will often counter propose a much higher premium that can be justified in accordance with the 1993 Act to allow room for negotiation.

The parties will usually agree a settlement premium which is somewhere in the middle of the section 42 or 13 figure and the section 45 or 21 Counter Notice figure. As you can see, it is therefore imperative for a landlord to be able to counter propose a higher figure, unless of course, he agrees with the tenant's initial proposal. As a result of Covid-19, the closure of offices and the world working remotely, there was a real concern within the industry that in the absence of enfranchisement surveyors being able to physically inspect flats (in cases under the 1993 Act) and houses (in the case of claims under the Leasehold Reform Act 1967) these counter notice deadlines could be missed.

Luckily, most of the cases I have worked on so far have not needed the parties to agree extensions for the deadlines set down by the Act. However, the ALEP Protocol is another welcome relief in this regard because it provides practitioners with the opportunity to request a reasonable extension for the time to serve any counter notice, if needed.

In reality however, where I have been required to serve counter notices, there has been no need to delay the service of the section 45 or 21 notice because physical valuations cannot be carried out. Most surveyors I work with have been able to undertake desktop valuations. On more complicated matters, the only caveat that expert surveyors may include is that their advice may be subject to change following a physical inspection once lockdown is over. It remains to be seen how that will affect negotiations going forward where circumstances change due to a physical inspection having taken place. Often, it is at inspection stage that the landlord discovers unauthorised alterations have taken place and so it will be interesting to see how this plays out once lockdown is eased (perhaps ask me in a few months' time!).

Like ALEP and the Law Society, the RICS issued guidance to its members on 15 May 2020 to allow RICS professionals and firms to provide services to their clients in line with UK Government Guidance. The RICS encouraged the use of remote valuations and implemented the recommended social distancing measures where physical inspections were necessary. Most surveyors I work with have remained busy during lockdown and have found that parties simply want to get the deals done.

This is pleasing as it means the pandemic hasn't stopped ongoing negotiations which were subject to physical inspections before the world went into lockdown.

The Tribunal System

Following the section above in which we discussed deadlines for service of notices, it would be remiss of me not to mention the next major deadline in enfranchisement; the deadline to reach agreement on the terms of acquisition.

In lease extensions and collective enfranchisement claims, the parties have a period of 6 months from service of the counter notice to agree terms of acquisition. For lease extension claims the terms of acquisition are the terms of the new lease and the premium pursuant to section 48(7) of the 1993 Act. For collective enfranchisements claims, the terms of acquisition are the terms of the transfer, apportionments and premium pursuant to section 24(8) of the 1993 Act.

If the terms of acquisition cannot be agreed within the requisite 6-month period then an application to the First-tier Tribunal (Property Chamber) ("FTT") is required in order to prevent the lease extension or collective enfranchisement claim from being deemed withdrawn. If an enfranchisement claim is deemed withdrawn, then the tenant(s) are statute barred from bringing another claim for a period of one year from the date of withdrawal. It is imperative that terms of acquisition are agreed or an application to the FTT made in advance of the deadline.

As a result of the ongoing Covid-19 crisis, Regional Tribunal Judge Powell suspended all directions relating to all ongoing tribunal applications on 19 March 2020 and on the same day the Senior President of the Tribunals, Sir Ernest Ryder issued a Practice Direction dealing with contingency arrangements for the FTT and Upper Tribunal in light of the pandemic.

The Practice Direction recognised that it may be necessary for tribunals to adjust their ways of working to limit the spread of coronavirus and therefore issued the practice direction on a pilot basis for a period of six months. This Practice Directions allows a salaried judge to decide whether cases be heard by a single judge or by a panel of fewer or different members than usual. The salaried judge will then make the decision if the case could not proceed or it would be subject to an unacceptable delay. This is all on the basis that the decision concurs with the overriding objective to enable the Tribunal to deal with cases fairly and justly and the parties' rights pursuant to European Court of Human Rights.

To be more efficient at dealing with cases the Practice Direction allows chamber presidents to 'triage' applications by permitting parties to produce photos and or videos of the condition of relevant aspects of the property and to undertake 'drive by' inspections.

The second practice direction issued on 26 March 2020 by Sir Ernest Ryder, applies to the FTT and provides guidance on how the Tribunal plans to operate whilst in lockdown.

The Southern and London Tribunal offices are, at the time of writing, currently closed but the Cambridge, Birmingham and Manchester offices are still open, albeit with reduced capacity. All correspondence and new applications are currently being made via the various email addresses provided in the guidance and the guidance has extended the time period for paying Tribunal fees by cheque or postal order to within 28 days of making the application.

Paying fees in this way poses a problem where, during lockdown, a firm's accounting team are now working from home. Helpfully, in a recent case I have submitted to the Tribunal via email, they have confirmed that once the application has been logged electronically onto the Tribunal's system, they will email details of where the fee can be paid electronically and thus avoiding the additional complication in dealing with payment by cheque or postal order. The Tribunal is therefore showing its flexibility to deal with the current circumstances by adopting more modern practices.

Face to face hearings or mediations are cancelled until further notice and no physical inspections are being carried out for at least six months. All current applications and appeals listed for face to face hearings up until the end of May 2020 were postponed, with a view to re-listing the hearings using remote technology or determining them by way of a paper hearing, with the consent of the parties.

Where directions were issued, the guidance implored parties to comply with the directions where possible but the Tribunal recognised that the impact of Covid-19 may affect the party's ability to comply with the directions. The guidance suggests that whilst the Tribunal will review directions already given, it is unlikely that they would start this process for at least six weeks.

Where an application had been made but no directions issued, then the Tribunal would consider the matter in due course, but again the Tribunal would be unlikely to issue directions for at least six weeks.

The Tribunal gave further guidance for cases that had already been heard, stating that there may be a delay in judgements being issued due to the pandemic.

Despite the guidance and in light of the difficulties faced by practitioners in meeting the deadlines ALEP went further and called on the government to extend the statutory timetables for determination by the Tribunal as laid down by the 1993 Act and the Commonhold and Leasehold Reform Act 2002 ("the 2002 Act") for right to manage claims during the pandemic.

In its letter to the Right Honorable Robert Buckland QC MP dated 26 March 2020 it called on the government to extend the statutory deadlines laid down by the 1993 Act and 2002 Act for filing applications to determine matters in dispute by 3 months once the lockdown period is over. ALEP urged the government to review the Tribunal process once the country returned to normal (or the new normal as we now call it) in order to update the processes and allow for a more modern way of working (for example, by allowing online applications and electronic payment of Tribunal fees).

At the time of writing, there has been no announcement by the government that the Tribunal process is to be reviewed after lockdown but the issues highlighted by ALEP are important and emphasize the need for a longer term review of the system. It is clear that there needs to be a way around these issues to help streamline applications and make them more efficient.

How has this affected those in practice

I recently had a case where the deadline to have all terms of acquisition agreed was fast approaching and it was apparent that the competent landlord in question was not able to confirm agreement. I therefore prepared the application for determination under section 48 of the 1993 Act and emailed off the application together with enclosures to the Southern First-tier Tribunal with a read and delivery receipt requested (together with a request for an acknowledgement of receipt in writing).

Seventy-two hours later and I had not received an acknowledgement from the Tribunal and so, in accordance with the Tribunal's guidance, I emailed to chase again. Luckily, I immediately received a response to confirm that my client's application had been received. Usually, I would send my application via special delivery or courier, obtain proof of delivery within 24 hours and then call to ensure that the Tribunal had received my application. Whilst remote and electronic working may have advanced the world of conveyancing and equity release as identified by Paul in the previous chapters, it seems to have slowed down the Tribunal. This is something that will need to change if we are to continue to work remotely and the Practice Direction and guidance issued by the Tribunal goes someway to achieving this.

However, for some of my clients, the delay at the Tribunal has been a blessing, it has provided the parties with more time to negotiate and agree on issues that prior to the pandemic, may have likely needed Tribunal intervention. However, for others it has only served to drag out matters even more which is frustrating and time consuming, and so now more than ever this Tribunal process is in need of modernisation.

The Future of Leasehold Enfranchisement

Stargazing at a forever moving target is quite difficult even for the best of us. Of course, I have not touched on the Law Commissions' proposed reforms of the enfranchisement sector, because quite frankly, I could write another book on the subject. In any event, it is anyone's guess as to whether Covid-19 has impacted on the Government's proposed program of reform.

However, I thought I would reflect on what Covid-19 has taught me about this area of law and what I anticipate for its future.

Despite an initial worry about incoming workload when we all went into lockdown, I have to say I have been pleasantly surprised by the appetite of leaseholders and landlords who want to use this time to maximise their property assets.

Whilst in lockdown, leaseholders have had the perfect opportunity to dust off their title deeds and take a look at the length of their lease and finally get round to speaking to specialists about how to extend the lease or even purchase their freehold with other leaseholders in the block.

ALEP reported a sharp rise in activity on their website during lockdown (almost 25% more traffic) meaning that leaseholders are using this time to search for solutions simply because they have the time to do so.

For some leaseholders, extending their lease can be one of those jobs on the list that they just never get around to. As the lease is a depreciating asset, the longer a leaseholder waits to extend their lease, the more expensive it will become. It is as simple as that and so waiting until the market normalises will not always the best option when it comes to leasehold.

The leasehold enfranchisement process can take some time and organisation to get off the ground. Now that some leaseholders have more time to think about how to better safeguard their leasehold assets, it is a good opportunity for them to consider their options and what can be done.

Even with social distancing measures in place, it is now easier than ever for leaseholders to set up video chats or messaging groups to stay in touch with their neighbours and other flat owners in order to organise a collective purchase of freeholds.

Even the lawyers and surveyors can join in to provide the much-needed assistance in guiding leaseholders through the complexity of collective enfranchisement.

Even if a statutory lease extension claim takes too long to complete, an informal deal could be done with the landlord. I am seeing a lot of landlords wanting to get deals through sooner rather than later in order to safeguard their own business interests. I anticipate seeing a lot of section 5 Landlord and Tenant Act 1987 deals coming through the door as landlords seek to dispose of their freehold reversions.

CHAPTER SIX
CONCLUSION

Firstly, thank you for taking the time to buy and read this book. I am sure it will probably horrify some of the people over the years that I am allowed to write books in the first place. What I say to them is, "surprise"! I wonder how those people are coping with the vast changes we are all making to our lives.

I have indicated in some of the early sections of this book that the world has changed. Some of it I would like to think is for the better. We should all now have more of an appreciation of certain things that we have not been able to do. I enjoy working at home but miss the office banter. I miss being able to meet my clients in person to discuss their legal issues as well as taking an interest in their lives as they do in mine. We have all had to change during these times.

If nothing else during this time it has shown me and I hope you the reader as well that things can be done in a different way. The law and its lawyers have often resisted change, "why fix something that is not broken" is a phrase one often hears. Well we have been forced to change and that is no bad thing in my opinion.

Thank you for taking the time to read this book. I shall hand over to Louise now for her to have the last word for once!

While I revel in getting in the last word, for once, I also want to thank you for reading this book and taking interest in our thoughts and views on our respective sectors.

Lockdown feels like it has gone on for an age, but, it has only really been a few months. Our industries have certainly changed within this short period of time and like Paul, I hope it is for the better.

Enfranchisement certainly has a way to go before it can class itself as being completely modernised and efficient but the changes and proposals I have guided you through in this book have shown that it is possible. We anticipate further hurdles to overcome once this area of law is reformed but if we can take anything positive from Covid-19 it is that it has forced us to improve, streamline and to grow for the better. Ultimately, it will be our clients that benefit from this transformation and in my mind that is certainly a very good thing.

MORE BOOKS BY
LAW BRIEF PUBLISHING

A selection of our other titles available now:-

'A Practical Guide to the General Data Protection Regulation (GDPR) – 2nd Edition' by Keith Markham
'Ellis on Credit Hire – Sixth Edition' by Aidan Ellis & Tim Kevan
'A Practical Guide to Working with Litigants in Person and McKenzie Friends in Family Cases' by Stuart Barlow
'Protecting Unregistered Brands: A Practical Guide to the Law of Passing Off' by Lorna Brazell
'A Practical Guide to Secondary Liability and Joint Enterprise Post-Jogee' by Joanne Cecil & James Mehigan
'A Practical Guide to the Pre-Action RTA Claims Protocol for Personal Injury Lawyers' by Antonia Ford
'A Practical Guide to Neighbour Disputes and the Law' by Alexander Walsh
'A Practical Guide to Forfeiture of Leases' by Mark Shelton
'A Practical Guide to Coercive Control for Legal Practitioners and Victims' by Rachel Horman
'A Practical Guide to Rights Over Airspace and Subsoil' by Daniel Gatty
'Tackling Disclosure in the Criminal Courts – A Practitioner's Guide' by Narita Bahra QC & Don Ramble
'A Practical Guide to the Law of Driverless Cars – Second Edition' by Alex Glassbrook, Emma Northey & Scarlett Milligan
'A Practical Guide to TOLATA Claims' by Greg Williams
'Artificial Intelligence – The Practical Legal Issues' by John Buyers
'A Practical Guide to the Law of Prescription in Scotland' by Andrew Foyle
'A Practical Guide to the Construction and Rectification of Wills and Trust Instruments' by Edward Hewitt
'A Practical Guide to the Law of Bullying and Harassment in the Workplace' by Philip Hyland

'A Practical Guide to Dog Law for Owners and Others' by Andrea Pitt
'RTA Allegations of Fraud in a Post-Jackson Era: The Handbook – 2nd Edition' by Andrew Mckie
'RTA Personal Injury Claims: A Practical Guide Post-Jackson' by Andrew Mckie
'On Experts: CPR35 for Lawyers and Experts' by David Boyle
'An Introduction to Personal Injury Law' by David Boyle
'A Practical Guide to Claims Arising From Accidents Abroad and Travel Claims' by Andrew Mckie & Ian Skeate
'A Practical Guide to Chronic Pain Claims' by Pankaj Madan
'A Practical Guide to Claims Arising from Fatal Accidents' by James Patience
'A Practical Approach to Clinical Negligence Post-Jackson' by Geoffrey Simpson-Scott
'Employers' Liability Claims: A Practical Guide Post-Jackson' by Andrew Mckie
'A Practical Guide to Subtle Brain Injury Claims' by Pankaj Madan
'A Practical Guide to Costs in Personal Injury Cases' by Matthew Hoe
'The No Nonsense Solicitors' Practice: A Guide To Running Your Firm' by Bettina Brueggemann
'The Queen's Counsel Lawyer's Omnibus: 20 Years of Cartoons from The Times 1993-2013' by Alex Steuart Williams

These books and more are available to order online direct from the publisher at www.lawbriefpublishing.com, where you can also read free sample chapters. For any queries, contact us on 0844 587 2383 or mail@lawbriefpublishing.com.

Our books are also usually in stock at www.amazon.co.uk with free next day delivery for Prime members, and at good legal bookshops such as Wildy & Sons.

We are regularly launching new books in our series of practical day-to-day practitioners' guides. Visit our website and join our free newsletter to be kept informed and to receive special offers, free chapters, etc.

You can also follow us on Twitter at www.twitter.com/lawbriefpub.

Printed in Poland
by Amazon Fulfillment
Poland Sp. z o.o., Wrocław

78375227R00047